WORLD OF
REPTILES

COBRAS

by Sophie Lockwood

Content Adviser: Harold K. Voris, PhD, Curator and Head, Amphibians and Reptiles, Department of Zoology, The Field Museum, Chicago, Illinois

THE CHILD'S WORLD®, CHANHASSEN, MINNESOTA

COBRAS

Published in the United States of America by The Child's World®
PO Box 326 • Chanhassen, MN 55317-0326 • 800-599-READ • www.childsworld.com

Acknowledgements:

The Child's World®: Mary Berendes, Publishing Director

Editorial Directions, Inc.: E. Russell Primm, Editorial Director; Pam Rosenberg, Editor; Judith Shiffer, Assistant Editor; Caroline Wood and Rory Mabin, Editorial Assistants; Susan Hindman, Copy Editor; Emily Dolbear and Sarah E. De Capua, Proofreaders; Elizabeth Nellums, Olivia Nellums, and Daisy Porter, Fact Checkers; Tim Griffin/IndexServ, Indexer; Cian Loughlin O'Day, Photo Researcher, Linda S. Koutris, Photo Editor

The Design Lab: Kathleen Petelinsek, Art Director, Cartographer; Julia Goozen, Page Production Artist

Photos:

Cover: Clive Druett / Papilio / Corbis; frontispiece / 4: Siede Preis / Photodisc / Getty Images.

Interior: Alamy Images: 11 (John Terence Turner), 21 (Peter van der Byl / wildlife), 22 (Norman Myers / Bruce Coleman Inc.), 29 (Steve Davy / La Belle Aurore); Animals Animals / Earth Scenes: 14 (McDonald Wildlife Photography), 35 (Erwin & Peggy Bauer); Corbis: 5-top left and 8 (Joe McDonald), 5-top right and 13, 5-bottom left and 36 (Roman Soumar), 16 (Martin Harvey), 27 (Archivo Iconografico S.A.), 31 (Wolfgang Kaehler), 32 (Jeffrey L. Rotman); Getty Images: 2-3 (Adam Jones / The Image Bank), 5-middle and 18 (Photodisc), 5-bottom right and 25 (Joel Simon / Stone).

Library of Congress Cataloging-in-Publication Data

Lockwood, Sophie.
Cobras / by Sophie Lockwood.
p. cm. — (The world of reptiles)
Includes bibliographical references (p.) and index.
ISBN 1-59296-544-X (library bound : alk. paper)
1. Cobras—Juvenile literature. I. Title.
QL666.O64L63 2006
597.96'42—dc22 2005024786

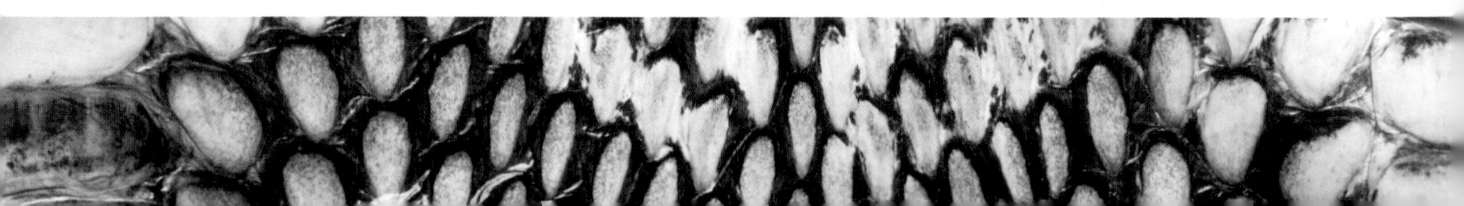

TABLE OF CONTENTS

Chapter One

In Etosha National Park

In Namibia, Africa, lies Etosha National Park, 8,600 square miles (22,274 square kilometers) of thornbush, grasslands, and desert. Namibia is nicknamed "the great big empty." Etosha means the "great white place" or "the place of dry water." These names describe the region accurately.

Each morning, elephants, ostriches, and wildebeests gather at the water hole to drink. Rhinos browse on the waving tall grasses. As the sun creeps higher, herds of antelope and zebras graze in the **savanna.** Vultures feed on the **carcass** of a dead warthog.

When night covers the park, an entirely different cast of creatures comes out. Bush babies with their bat-shaped ears and bushy tails cry from their perches in thorn trees. Black-backed jackals scavenge through garbage left by campers. A leopard growls loudly as he hunts for stray antelope.

Did You Know?
Cobras are one of the few snakes in the world that can spit their **venom.**

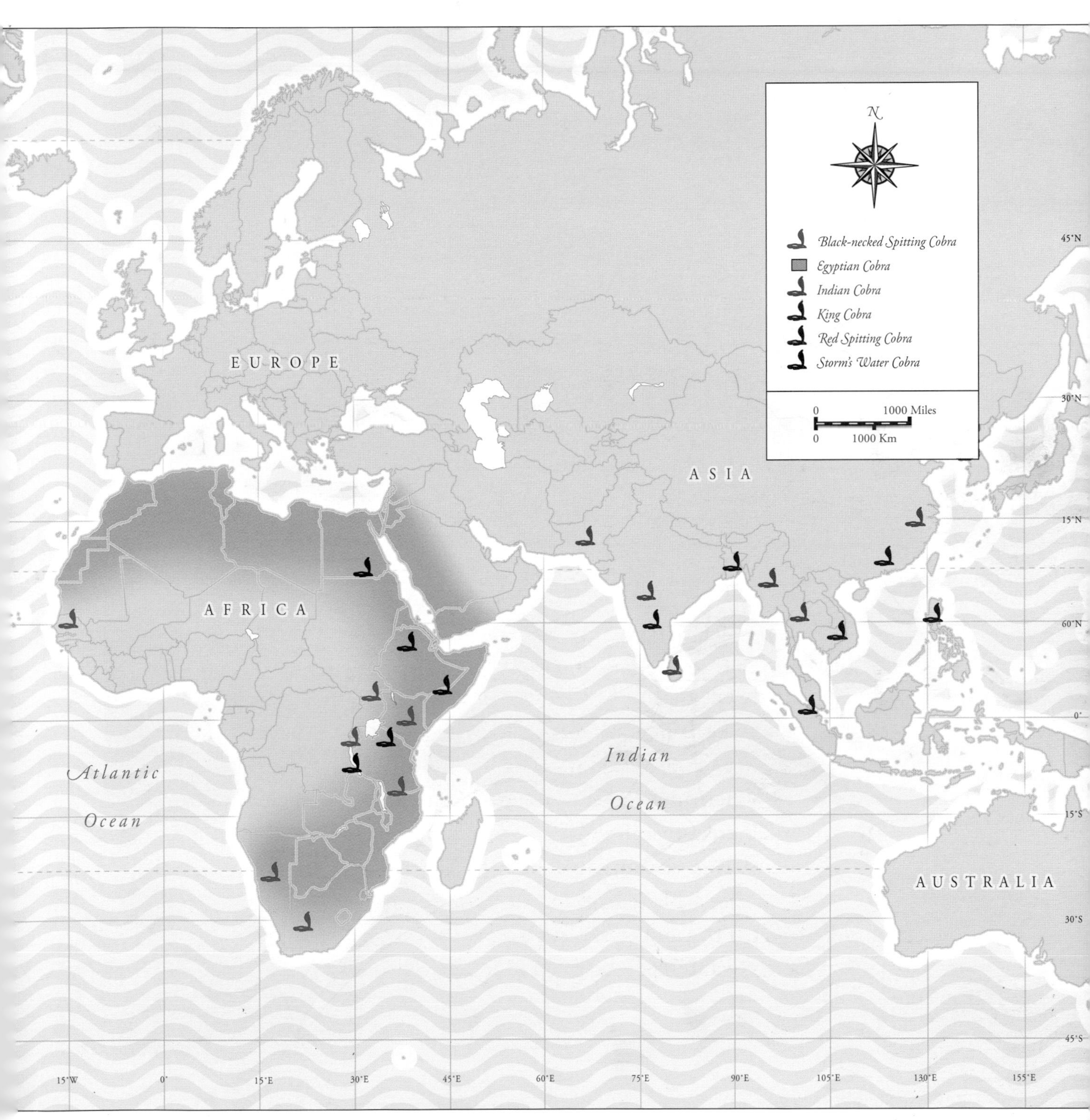

Cobras live thoughout Africa, the Middle East, and South Asia extending all the way to East Asia.

Another creature is also on the hunt. It slips through the grasses without a sound. It is a black-necked spitting cobra. This adult male measures not quite 6 feet (1.8 meters) long. He is hungry and it's dinnertime.

A black-necked spitting cobra aims at its victim's eyes and can spit its venom as far as 10 feet (3 m).

A herd of common duikers, which are small antelope, surprises the cobra. It rises up and takes aim. A spitting cobra can spit its venom accurately for about 10 feet (3 m). An unlucky duiker gets a dose of cobra venom in its eyes. The venom is painful and causes temporary blindness. The injured duiker tries to flee. The rest of the herd runs away toward a stand of acacia.

The cobra approaches a marshy hollow. He senses movement among the reeds. It is a cane rat, an ideal meal. Cane rats are considered excellent eating—even by humans.

The snake strikes. Its fangs inject venom into the rat, and the rat is paralyzed. The cobra unhinges his jaws and begins to swallow the rat whole. It goes down headfirst.

The cobra returns to an empty termite hill. Black-necked spitting cobras make their homes in hollow trees, felled tree trunks, abandoned termite mounds, and anthills. Sometimes a spitting cobra will eat a rat, then move into the rat's hole—a meal and a new home with one quick bite.

Black-necked Spitting Cobra Fast Facts

(Naja nigricollis nigricollis)

Adult length: 4 to 6.6 feet (1.2 to 2 m)

Coloration: Black neck with a grayish body

Range: Eastern Africa, Kenya, Uganda, Tanzania, Rwanda, Burundi, Senegal, Namibia, and South Africa

Reproduction: 10 to 24 eggs per nest

Diet: Rodents, small birds, toads, lizards, and snakes

Chapter Two

Packed with Poison

Cobras belong to the reptile family called Elapidae. The family is made up of venomous snakes, including coral snakes, cobras, kraits, sea snakes, and mambas. Cobras are known as venomous snakes because their bites are packed with poison. A cobra's venom attacks the nervous system of its victims and paralyzes them. Other than the venom **sacs** in the head, however, there is no poison in a cobra. Surprisingly, they make good eating and taste a bit like chicken.

There are many different species of cobra. The largest is the king cobra, which can grow to about 18 feet (5.5 m) long. King cobras are the largest venomous snakes in the world. They are not, however, larger than pythons, anacondas, or boa constrictors, which are not venomous.

Most cobras belong to the genus *Naja*. These cobras live in savannas, near wetlands, or in forests. They are medium-sized snakes, from 4 to 6 feet (1.2 to 1.8 m) in length. Rodents, small birds, other snakes, lizards, toads, and frogs are their favorite prey.

Would You Believe?
Cobras can inject enough venom in a single bite to kill an elephant. One gram (0.035 ounce) of cobra venom can kill fifty adult humans.

Some cobras prefer unusual habitats—at least, unusual for cobras. Two types of water cobras live in western Africa. They spend most of their active time in the water, and they sleep and nest onshore. The Arabian Peninsula has a desert cobra, and two species of African cobras prefer to live in trees.

VENOM AND FANGS

In a small village in India, a teenage boy goes to the family rice supply. His mind is on the soccer goal he scored yesterday. He is careless when he reaches into the grain hut. He should have looked first.

Coiled among the sacks of rice is an Indian cobra. Also called an Asian cobra, this snake is drawn to villages and human homes because it eats mice and rats. Grain storage huts attract rodents, and cobras follow close behind.

Startled, the cobra hisses, then strikes. The boy has gotten a full dose of cobra venom. Unfortunately, the village

A king cobra will flare its hood and stand upright when it is threatened.

is far from a hospital and the medicine that would save his life. Thousands of Indians die from cobra bites every year. Yet Indians rarely kill cobras because they consider them to be sacred.

Cobra fangs are hollow. They are attached to venom sacs in the snake's head. Adult cobras can control the amount of venom they deliver per bite. **Juvenile** cobras cannot. For this reason, some people claim that juveniles are more deadly than adults. In some ways, cobra venom is like human saliva. It is produced in sacs or cavities—like human salivary glands—in the head. After a bite, the cobra's body automatically makes more venom, just like your salivary glands produce more saliva.

A cobra's fangs are attached to a bone that can rotate slightly. This allows the fangs to point forward when necessary. But the fangs normally point back into the mouth so the snake doesn't bite itself. This is also helpful for eating. A cobra swallows its prey whole. If its

Indian Cobra Fast Facts
(Naja naja)
Adult length: 6 to 7 feet (1.8 to 2.1 m)
Coloration: Black bands and eyes; black, dark brown, and white body; half-rings on the underside of the hood
Range: India, Central Asia, and Southeast Asia
Reproduction: 8 to 45 eggs per nest
Diet: Rodents, lizards, and frogs

The Indian cobra is sometimes called the spectacled cobra because of the two black spots that appear on its neck when it flares its hood.

fangs were permanently pointing outward, the snake could not gulp down a mouse or a chicken so easily.

Cobras, like most other snakes, eat animals that are much larger than their mouths. They detach their jaws to open their mouths wider. Slippery saliva coats the prey so that it slides down more easily. The saliva jump-starts the digestive process. It can take several days for a cobra to digest a meal. Typically, cobras eat rodents, lizards, other snakes, small birds, toads, and frogs. Water cobras eat fish because they spend most of their time in water. King cobras eat mostly snakes. They even eat other cobras!

SMOOTH SKIN, EXPANDING HOOD

As a cobra grows, its skin becomes too tight to live in. To remove it, the snake scrapes its body against a rock or tree bark. Juvenile cobras change their skins nearly every month during their first year of life. Occasionally, juveniles eat their shed skins. Adult cobras get new skins four to six times a year. Changing from one skin to another takes about two weeks.

Although the cobra gets bigger, the number of scales on its body remains the same. The placement and pattern of those scales do not change, but with age

An Indian cobra eats a rodent. Cobras swallow their prey whole.

Did You Know?
A cobra's sense of smell comes from a special organ in the roof of the snake's mouth, called the Jacobson's organ. The Jacobson's organ has two highly sensitive hollows, like human sinuses. This organ improves the sense of smell and allows cobras to track both prey and future mates.

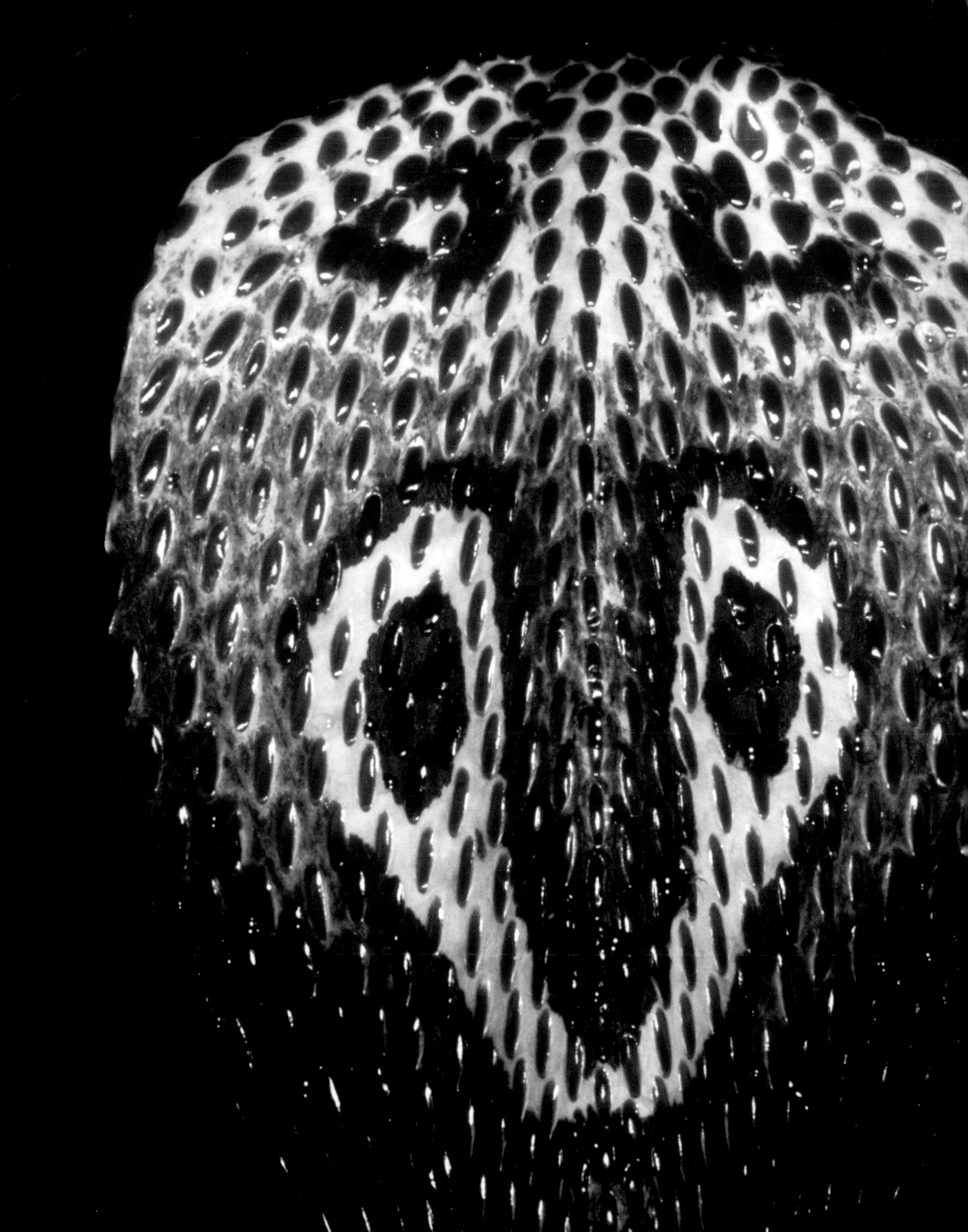

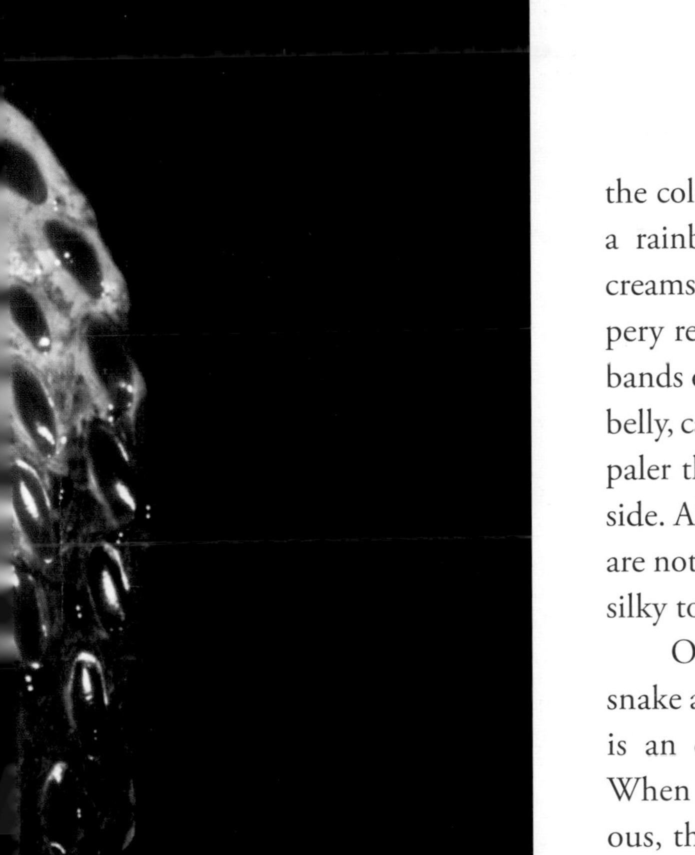

the colors may differ. Cobras come in a rainbow of colors: pinks, yellows, creams, whites, grays, browns, coppery reds, and blacks. They may have bands or spots or speckles. The snake's belly, called the **ventral** side, is usually paler than its back, called the **dorsal** side. Although cobras look slimy, they are not. Cobra skins are dry, slick, and silky to touch.

One feature that identifies a snake as a cobra is its hood. The hood is an extension of the cobra's ribs. When frightened, excited, or curious, the cobra expands its hood. The hood's dorsal side often features a spectacle pattern that looks like eyes behind eyeglasses. These patterns are probably there to frighten away **predators.**

Cobras can often be identified by the markings on their hoods. A cobra that displays its hood is letting other animals—humans included—know that it is ready to defend itself!

Did You Know?
Baby cobras have full-strength venom and can kill a human within a few hours of hatching.

which is good because the mother takes no part in feeding her young. Hatchlings eat small creatures, such as insects, frogs, toads, and mice. By the time they become adults, king cobras feed mostly on snakes. A very big king cobra can easily swallow a snake 6 feet (1.8 m) long. Their eating habits gave king cobras their scientific name, *Ophiophagus hannah*—"snake eater."

DAYTIME . . . NIGHTTIME

Some cobras are active by day and others hunt by night. Asia's king cobra and Africa's Cape cobras are **diurnal,** active during the day. Cape cobras feed on frogs, toads, lizards, and snakes. These prey usually sun themselves in the day and retreat to a burrow or nest at night, so Cape cobras hunt when their prey are active.

Most cobras, however, are **nocturnal.** They are active at night. Egyptian cobras, red spitting cobras, and snouted cobras, for example, are nighttime hunters. Red spitting cobras are small, thin cobras, usually measuring between 28 and 48 inches (71 to 122 cm) long. They are common in Tanzania and Kenya. During the daytime, they hide in termite hills, fallen trees, or tree hollows. Although they prefer frogs for dinner, red spitting cobras are **cannibals** and have been known to eat juveniles

of their own species. This may explain why juvenile red spitting cobras are active during the day, while their parents are active at night.

A TYPICAL COBRA LIFE

Cobras, like all reptiles, have no internal control over their body temperatures. They are cold-blooded creatures. They sun themselves to get warm and find shade to stay cool. In very cold weather, they do not move about much. A cold snake is a sluggish snake.

Many scientists consider the Cape cobra the most dangerous African cobra species. A bite from this snake can kill a human in as little as thirty minutes.

An Indian cobra confronts a mongoose. The mongoose is one of the only animals that has a chance of winning a battle with a cobra.

The cobra's daily life mixes hunting and resting. The larger the snake is, the larger the food it will eat. Once a meal is swallowed, the snake must rest. It may take days to digest a large meal, and the snake remains inactive during that time.

The more food a young snake eats, the faster it grows and the safer it is from predators. Juvenile cobras face danger from mongooses, **ratels,** birds of prey, and other snakes. As adults, only the ratel and the mongoose have a chance against the cobra.

A cobra's ability to reproduce depends more on its size than on its age. Generally, when a cobra reaches half its maximum length, it can produce young. For a king cobra, that happens at about five years. For smaller cobras, reproductive age might come at two years or older. Most cobras lay their eggs in tunnel-shaped holes, rotting trees, or empty termite hills. The number of eggs per nest depends on the species. Older, larger females can lay more eggs than smaller, younger females.

If all goes well, a cobra will live about twenty years in the wild. They live longer in captivity because they don't have to face the threats that wild cobras face. A zoo cobra doesn't worry about being trampled by herds of wildebeest. It won't be scooped up by an eagle or run over by a truck.

Chapter Four

Snake Charmers

In Sri Lanka, a man with a turban carries a bamboo flute and a covered basket. He spreads a blanket on a street corner, sits on the ground, and tips the lid off the basket. Then he picks up his flute and plays. Slowly, a deadly cobra emerges from the basket. A crowd gathers around the show.

The snake sways back and forth as the snake charmer plays. It hisses and swiftly strikes out at the man. The crowd shies away in fear. They know that cobra bites are deadly. The snake charmer continues playing as though nothing has happened.

What makes the cobra dance? No one is sure. It is not the music. Cobras have a poor sense of hearing. They have no outer eardrums. The snake may pick up vibrations of the flute. It may also sway to the side-to-side movement of the flute as it is played.

Why isn't the snake charmer concerned about the bite? Snake charmers are not stupid. They collect cobras while the snakes are sleepy and slow. The first thing charmers do after catching a snake is remove the snake's

A snake charmer performs with his cobra in Delhi, India.

venom sacs. The bite received during the show was annoying—but not dangerous.

ANCIENT EGYPT

People honored and feared cobras in ancient Egypt. Heka, the god of magic, was depicted as a human with a snake's head. The Pharaoh, Egypt's ruler, wore a crown with a gold-and-jeweled cobra's head. The cobra represented the pharaoh's power over life and death. Even the Egyptian *Book of the Dead* shows a cobra as a symbol of the earth.

Artists carved statues and painted pictures of cobras to decorate Egyptian tombs. This isn't surprising because the venom-packed bites of Egyptian cobras put many people in those tombs. In ancient Egypt, healers were expected to know spells and potions to overcome snakebites. Unfortunately, healers had little success against cobra venom.

INDIA'S COBRAS

About five thousand years ago, the ancient people of India believed in a group of serpent people called Nagas. The Nagas were supposed to be snakes that took on human form. Nagas were not mere mortals; they were gods.

Hindu people have honored cobras for centuries. Cobras are still respected

Did You Know?
Legend says that Cleopatra died from the bite of an asp. Though an asp is a particular kind of snake, the word *asp* was used in ancient times to mean any snake. In truth, the snake that killed Cleopatra was most likely an Egyptian cobra.

The gold coffin of pharaoh Psusennes shows him wearing a crown with a cobra's head.

and worshipped. Throughout India, the people celebrate the festival of snakes, Nag-Panchami. In the Punjab region, special dough is made using flour and butter collected from every household. The dough is shaped like a cobra. Leaders parade through the town carrying the dough in a basket. Then the cobra image is buried. Everyone participates, hoping that paying honor to the cobra will protect family members from being bitten.

In Maharashta, Hindu women bathe and dress in special saris to celebrate the cobra. On Nag-Panchami, they place bowls of milk in places where cobras are known to visit.

Some Indians keep mongooses to protect them from cobras. The mongoose moves quickly. Its thick fur protects it from the cobra's venom. In a battle between a cobra and a mongoose, the mongoose usually wins.

COBRA MEDICINES

The Irula tribe of India once worshipped cobras. They believed that cobras were the source of their tribe's wealth because, for many years, the people survived by capturing cobras and selling their skins. In 1978, the Indian government banned the sale

Egyptian Cobra Fast Facts
(Naja haje)
Adult length: 3 to 6 feet (1 to 1.8 m)
Coloration: Varies, including yellows, creams, grays, browns, coppery-red, black; dark spots over body; black bands
Range: Africa and the Middle East
Reproduction: 8 to 33 eggs per nest
Diet: Toads, tortoises, lizards, snakes, small mammals, birds, and fish

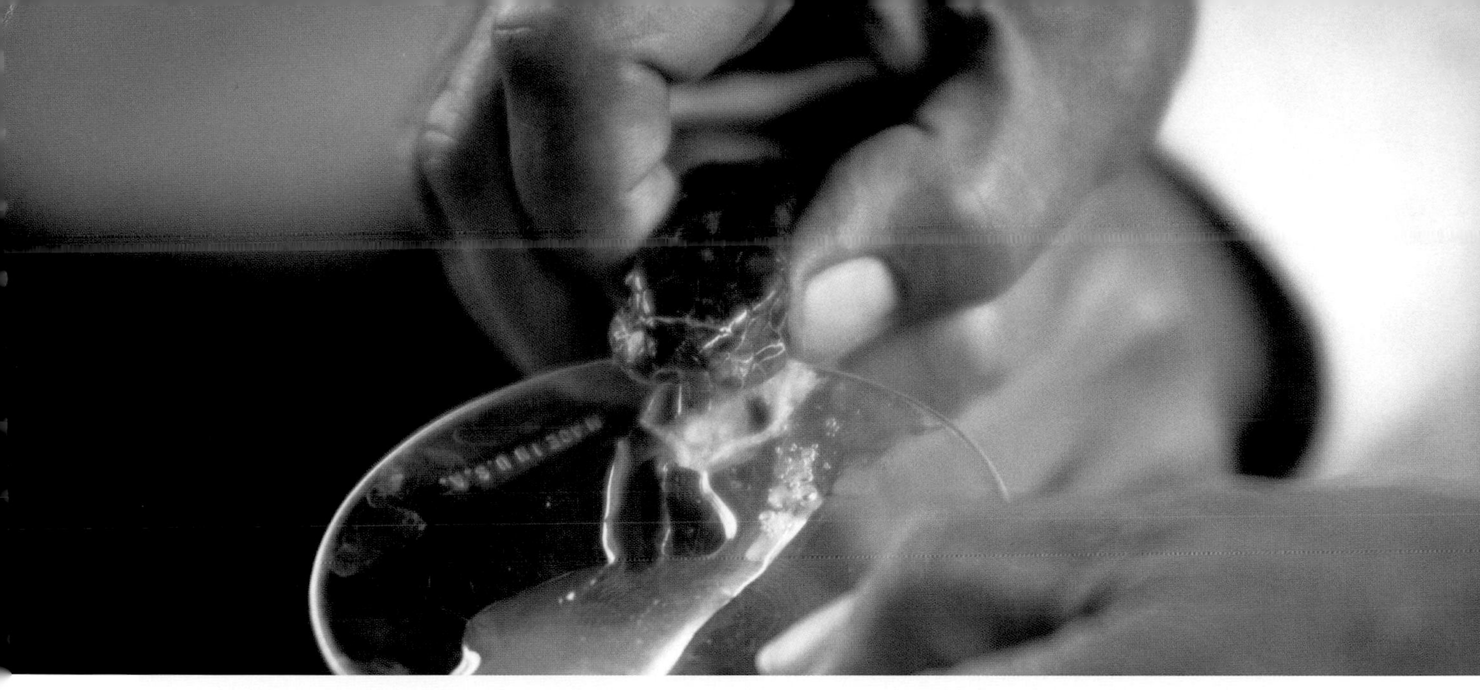

of cobra skins. The Irula needed to find a new way to earn money. Today, they catch cobras and milk their venom.

Cobra venom has been used for medicine in many cultures. The venom acts naturally on the nervous system. Traditional healers used cobra venom to ease pain from arthritis and rheumatism.

Today, medical researchers are studying the potential for cobra venom to be used as a pain reliever. A small dose of cobra venom has three to four times the pain-relieving power of morphine. Doctors hope that cobra venom may be used to treat heart problems, pain, cancerous tumors, and leprosy. The venom is also used to produce antivenin, the **antidote** for cobra bites. Unfortunately, most hospitals that carry the antidote are not close enough to the places where cobras roam.

Read It!
The mongoose is a natural enemy of cobras and the basis for an entertaining story. Read Rudyard Kipling's *Rikki-Tikki-Tavi,* available in most public libraries.

A handler milks a cobra's venom at a snake park in Thailand.

Chapter Five

Humans and Cobras

Cobras and other snake species are big business across Southeast Asia. The demand for meat in China has people purchasing tons of snakes, turtles, rats, lizards, and tortoises. While these meats may not appear on many American restaurant menus, eating snake for supper is destroying the cobra populations of Thailand, Burma, Vietnam, and other Southeast Asian nations. These animals are also popular for use in making traditional medicines in Asia.

Despite international laws against the sale of endangered species and their body parts, king cobra meat is sold at open markets. A trip to Bangkok's farmers' market proves it. Legal protection and legal enforcement are far apart when it comes to saving endangered reptiles.

While there are many benefits to dead cobras, there is a price to pay for killing off snake populations: more rats and mice. All the mousetraps in the world cannot compete with snakes for efficient rodent control. In areas where cobra populations are seri-

Did You Know?
A group of cobras is called a quiver—just like a group of arrows. Do you think that is because they are shaped like arrows? Or is it because they are just as deadly?

A cobra skin is stretched out to dry outside a hut in Thailand.

ously reduced, rat populations are rapidly on the rise. Rats and mice can eat their way through a year's grain crop in no time. Rodents leave waste behind that fouls remaining food supplies. It might be worth putting up with the cobras to avoid a plague of rats.

Cobras face three main threats in the wild: loss of habitat, overhunting by humans, and predators. Loss of habitat is easy to explain and hard to fix. The areas in

Decreasing populations of cobras and other snakes often leads to overpopulation of rodents, such as these rats in Rajasthan, India.

Asia where cobras are common have large human populations. As the number of people increases, their needs also expand. They need places to live, water to drink, ways to travel, and food to eat.

Humans get more living, farming, and traveling space by getting rid of wilderness. In Sri Lanka, home of Indian cobras, people clear land using a method called slash and burn. They cut down the trees for timber and burn away all the brush. This practice destroys cobra habitats. The land is turned into farmland, and cobras have no place to hunt except human homes and storage huts.

Building roads creates a different problem for cobras. Being cold-blooded animals, cobras sun themselves to get warm. Black tarmac gets toasty warm, so a cobra will coil up for a snooze and then get squashed by a truck on the highway. Even if cobras did not sun themselves on roads, they would need to cross them for food. When car meets cobra, the cobra loses.

Overhunting is the greatest threat to cobras. While ratels and mongooses prey on cobras, their impact on cobra populations is small. Humans are the cobra's worst enemy. They can catch cobras easily. The snakes may have a powerful bite, but they are slow and sluggish, particularly in cold weather. People

Storm's Water Cobra Fast Facts

(Boulengerina annulata stormsi)

Adult length: 4 to 5 feet (1.2 to 1.5 m)

Coloration: Yellowish gray to bluish; 2 to 3 distinct black bands on neck

Range: Shores of Lake Tanganyika

Reproduction: Unknown

Diet: Fish, toads, and frogs

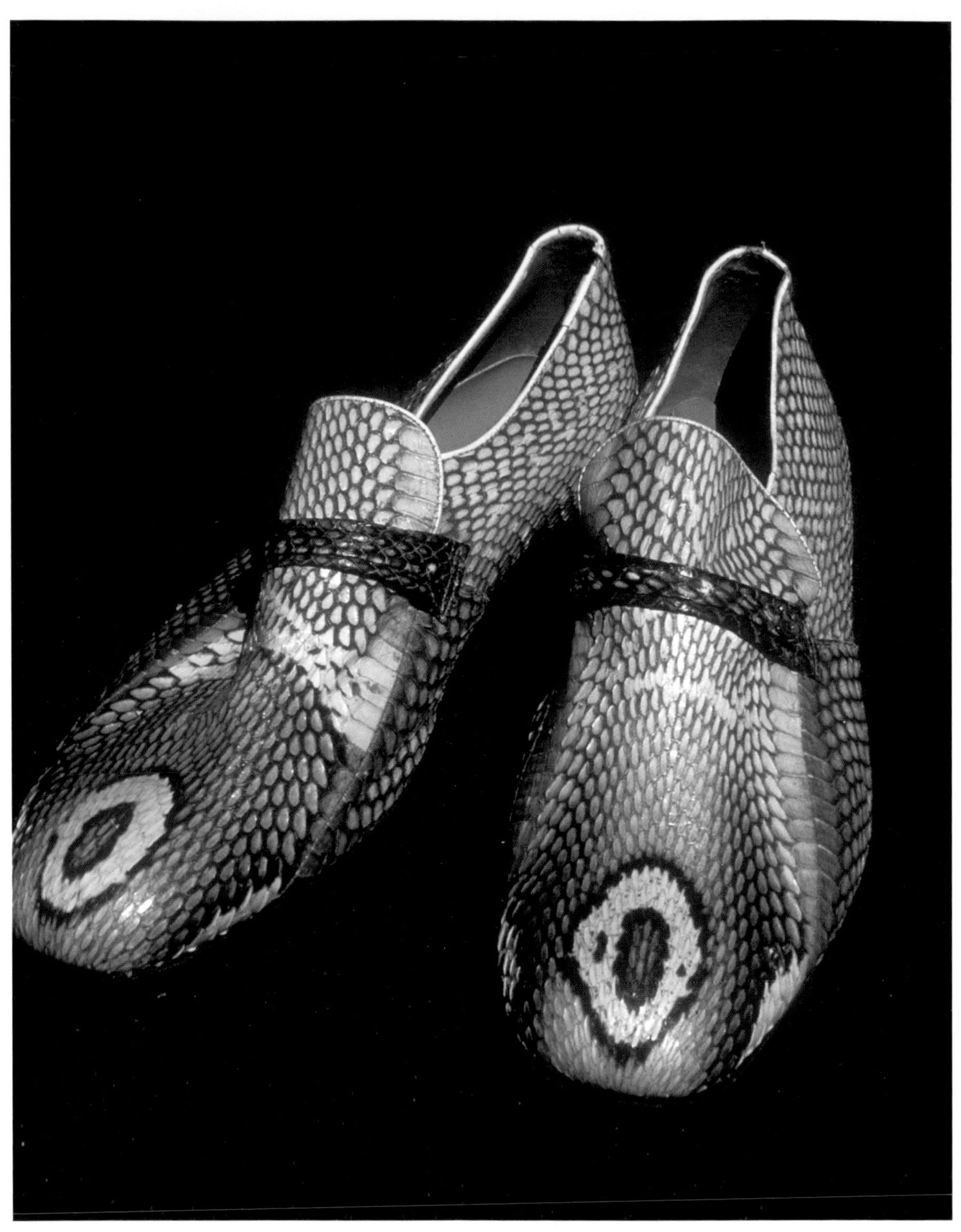

Cobras skins have been used to make shoes, such as these cobra skin loafers. Because cobras are on the endangered species list, using skins to make shoes and other items is illegal.

hunt cobras for their skins and meat. Many cobra skins are not particularly attractive, but banded cobras, such as the Storm's water cobra, have beautiful, distinctive skins. Belts, hatbands, wallets, and purses from these skins are expensive—and illegal.

Cobras have been on the endangered species list for years. The most endangered cobra is the king cobra, and it truly needs protection. Other cobra species have varying populations. They are grouped together for legal protection because scientists believe that most people can't tell one cobra from another.

The Thai cobra should probably not be listed because its population numbers are quite healthy. There are other reasons, however, to protect the species. Doctors have discovered that Thai cobra venom has a chemical compound that helps control the human immune system. The drug may help people survive after a kidney, liver, heart, lung, or bone marrow transplant. Normally, human bodies might reject new transplanted organs, but serum with the Thai cobra venom compound may help prevent that. Thai cobra venom could actually save lives.

For many years, China plundered Vietnam's cobra population. Adult cobras were killed for their meat and for body parts to make traditional medicines. The cobra

population suffered, and the Vietnamese people saw little benefit from the slaughter.

Some clever Vietnamese have decided to turn plunder into profit. The Vinh Son **Commune** near Hanoi is farming cobras. The commune hired a cobra specialist to help them breed and raise cobras. Nine out of ten cobra eggs hatch successfully on the commune, producing many thousands of snakes per year.

Once juvenile cobras reach adult size, they are slaughtered and the meat and skins sold. This is just like cattle,

Cobras are often used in traditional medicines, such as these bottles of cobra elixir from Vietnam.

chicken, or sheep farms in North America. The cobra farm provides jobs and money for its workers.

In the future, the commune hopes to release some of its cobras into the wild each year. The ideal situation would be releasing the cobras in a national park or preserve. **Conservation** specialists must consider all aspects of such a move. Most important is whether farmed cobras will be able to fend for themselves in the wild.

Conservation is a tricky business. Lots of people want to preserve cuddly koalas, majestic tigers, and humanlike chimpanzees. Few people line up to save snakes. But nature is a careful balance of plants and animals. When humans destroy that balance, all nature suffers. Nature preserves, wilderness areas, zoos, and captive breeding farms may help counter some species' losses in the wild.

The medicine that cures cancer or reduces pain may come from cobra venom. Snakes are the best means of controlling rat and mouse populations. And the food that feeds growing human populations in the future may come from farmed cobras. Every creature has a role in nature—even cobras.

Glossary

antidote (AN-ti-dote) a medical remedy for a poison

cannibals (KAN-uh-buhlz) animals that eat the young of their own species

carcass (KAR-kuhss) the body of a dead animal

clutch (KLUHCH) a group of eggs laid at one time

commune (KOM-yoon) a farm or business in which the workers are also the owners

conservation (kon-sur-VAY-shuhn) the act of saving or preserving some aspect of wildlife

diurnal (dye-UR-nuhl) active in the daytime

dorsal (DOR-suhl) an animal's back

hatchling (HACH-ling) a newborn that emerges from an egg

juvenile (JOO-vuh-nuhl) a young animal, like a human toddler

nocturnal (nok-TUR-nuhl) active in the nighttime

predators (PRED-uh-turz) animals that hunt and kill other animals for food

ratels (RAH-tuhlz) mammals found in Africa and Asia that resemble a badger

sacs (SAKS) containers or wrappings

savanna (suh-VAN-uh) a tropical grassland

venom (VEN-uhm) a poisonous substance produced by some snakes

ventral (VEN-truhl) the underside of a snake or other creature

For More Information

Watch It

Cobra: The King of Snakes. VHS (Silver Spring, Md., Discovery Channel, 2004).

The Crocodile Hunter: Spitting Cobras of the World. VHS (Silver Spring, Md., Discovery Channel, 2000).

Read It

Eckart, Edana. *King Cobra.* Danbury, Conn.: Children's Press, 2003.

Kipling, Rudyard. *Rikki-Tikki-Tavi.* Mankato, Minn.: Creative Education, 1986.

Taylor, Barbara. *Cobras.* Austin, Tex.: Raintree Steck-Vaughn, 2003.

Look It Up

Visit our home page for lots of links about cobras:
http://www.childsworld.com/links

Note to Parents, Teachers, and Librarians: We routinely verify our Web links to make sure they are safe, active sites—so encourage your readers to check them out!

The Animal Kingdom
Where Do Cobras Fit In?

Kingdom: Animal
Phylum: Chordata
Class: Reptilia
Order: Squamata
Family: Elapidae
Genus/Species: There are dozens of cobra species.

Index

About the Author

Sophie Lockwood is a former teacher and a longtime writer. She writes textbooks, newspaper articles, and magazine articles. Sophie enjoys writing about animals and their habits. The most interesting part of her research, Sophie says, is learning how scientists apply their knowledge to save endangered species. She lives with her husband in the foothills of the Blue Ridge Mountains.